the Blomidon Logs

Deirdre Dwyer

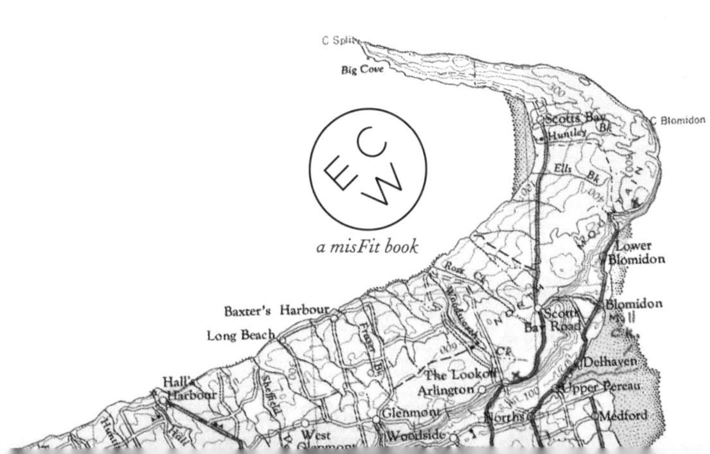

ECW
a misFit book

VER ST LAWRENCE
ISLAND OF ANTICOSTI
GASPE
BAY OF CHALEUR
GULF O
NEW BRUNSWICK
NORTHUMBERLAND STRAIT
PRINCE EDWARD ISLAN
BAY OF FUNDY
NOVA SCOTIA
Douglas
Richmond
Bonaventure
Dalhousie
Bathurst
Newcastle
Douglastown
Chatham
Grand Falls
Woodstock
Houlton
Stanley
Tay
FREDERICTON
Oromocte
Kingston
ST JOHN
Carleton
St Stephens
Calais
St Andrews
Machias
Lit Machias
Columbia
Harrington
Moncton
Dorchester
Amherst
Waterford
Ramsheg
Parsboro
Londonderry
Cornwallis
Horton
Falmouth
Windsor
Newport
Wilmot
Bridgetown
Annapolis
Digby
Weymouth
New Edinburgh
HALIFAX
Dartmouth
Liverpool
Yarmouth
Shelburne
Barrington
Tryon
St Davids
New London
CHARLOTTE TOWN

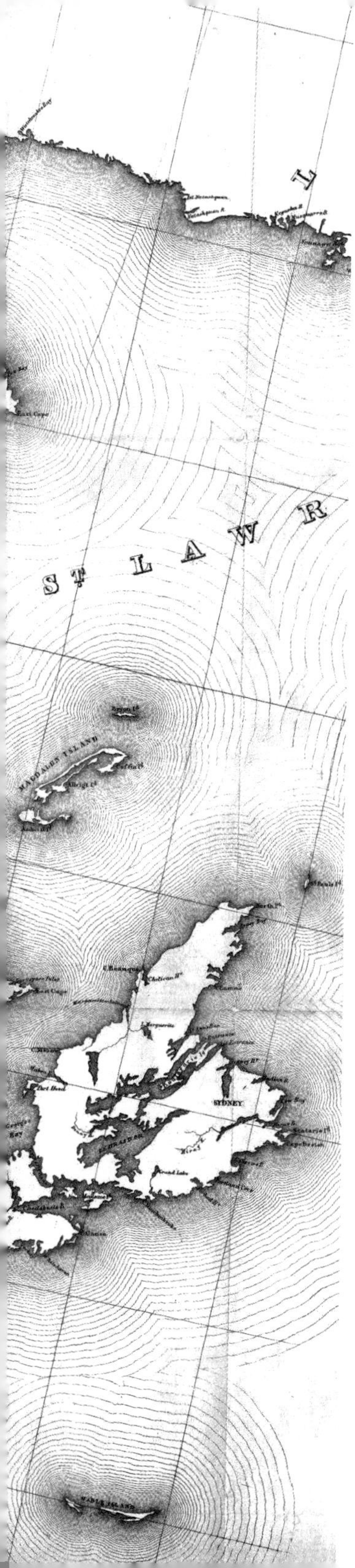

To my parents, Bea and Dave,
with love and thanks for Blomidon
and other legacies

ARCHIVES

DRAMATIS PERSONAE

THE KIDS

"us": John, Dee, Kay, Ian, & Ann Dwyer

Nancy, Doc, & Jerry Bigelow

Johnny & Alan Legge
& an older sister

Bill & Garfield Lyons
& several older sisters

Dan & Mark Legge
& an older brother and sister

THE ADULTS

Dwight (Skip) & Arley Bigelow:
Nancy's parents

(Bouk) & Theresa Legge:
Johnny & Alan's parents

(Hun) & Marion Lyons:
Bill & Garfield's parents

Irlyn (Ike) & Connie Legge:
Dan & Mark's parents

Bert & Gloria Green:
& their children.

THE OLD CABIN

GLOOSCAP AND HIS MAGIC

The book at bedtime—
my parents read to us
when we were more than seasons
away from the Great Chief.

He strolls out on the first page,
a loon on his shoulder,
with a tall staff, a smile,
his braids curled like two thick earrings.

By his side, two wolves:
the dark one on a rock howls
a story to the animal world,
a summons.

The other lowers his head,
scowls at troublemakers, any dark force.

When my father returned
he said he found a ring of stones.
Oh, where thy wigwam stood tall.

I believe in Glooscap
who came from the sky
in his stone canoe.

The Great Chief who fought the Ice King,
year-round winter,
fought the giant Famine
and Badger, sometimes a man.

Glooscap brought the Queen of Summer
for six months
as we rally, eager,
to meet her at Blomidon.

THE FIRST LOGBOOK

(JUNE 1964–SEPTEMBER 1970)

"Hunting" is all
he's written, my father alone,
five October days at the old camp,
and setting his steps quietly
down on the fall envelope
of a wooded path.

"Camp Glooscap": he pays tribute
on the first page to the Great Chief.

The short entries, the slender
black book. Unwritten are the lean years,
the war years, and before
as if history's pen had not yet
been carved.

And the barrel of mountain water
is found only in the foliage
of a photograph; its cold
ancient taste says nothing
of the short entry

when we arrive: 4:30, July 15
'66. A year later my first words
in the log, of hiking back to Indian Springs.

We grow the words of summer.

REQUESTED

We always asked for the story
of the fat Giant of Seasons, Coolpujot,
always turned to him cross-eyed:
sprawling rolls of his tummy,
press of his wide arm
as Glooscap wields a crowbar—
to roll the giant over.

He'll defeat the Ice King's
charm where the Great Chief sleeps
for six cold months.

When Coolpujot turns over
he warms the world.

Night, wind climbs
down the mountain. Maybe
the fire listens when we ask
for stories of *swamp-soggins*

with bulky feet as long
as snowshoes. Can you hear
that damp oozing sound?

And the chunk and chew,
the mangle, spitting out of shrubs
by *side-hill gougers* with one short
leg, the other long and loose.

And even in town in daylight
we listen, look up for *Wolfville birds*
that bark and spread wide wings
over a tree-lined sky.

THE OTHER CHILD, GOING THERE

The surplus of summer: Mom and boxes in the kitchen, Dad in the driveway carefully packing the trunk. Later the youngest cradled in the front while the four of us in the back tease, wrestle anticipation: another fidgety child, my invisible sister. We stop for donuts. I like the chocolate ones with lemon where the hole should be. She gulps hers down, pokes at us to be off; at the Uniacke House rolls her eyes, slips into roped-off chambers. "Don't jump on the . . ."—crack of slats, crash, and she scurries away, doesn't look back as staff confer.

When we slow for the full face of the house we call haunted—grey boards, crooked shutters—she sulks. The sister my parents can't see. Somewhere we eat ice cream; Ian loses a tooth in the soft kind, maybe biting on anticipation's presumption and grit. Above the Avon: filigree of the widow's walk. She surprises, feeds me stories of women: sombre dress, yoke of dark lace, as if she's known them through their yearning. Lunch under a canopy in Grand-Pré: chowder, scones for adults; for us: hamburgers with relish and ketchup she drips.

And when we crest the hill, lounge
in our gaze at the Cape across the basin,
she dances, squirms,
pleads with us, when we go
beyond that moment
where she, resplendent,
would have us wait.

ANOTHER LANDMARK ON THE WAY

The grandest, most elaborate house
in town a sleeping castle
with climbing wisteria, deliberate
shrubs, a tall privet hedge

had us cloistered around questions:
Who are they? What do they keep
from us? What have they done,
in their prestigious absence, with time?

                                        It's as if the car
is slowed by contemplation,
nineteenth century thought, the anachronism
of its machine.

Canning, the town should take back
its early name, Apple Tree Landing:
ships would dock again,
box bins full of McIntosh, Gravenstein
would fill the hold.

                                        Does every house
have cubbyholes, tunnels,
a desk with a secret drawer?

Its brown paint is sombre
and ivy grows unusually quick,
winds itself like a shroud
and climbs like a ladder up the tower window

so we'll never know if a young girl
meanders those halls and dreams
of apples unloaded in sweltering Brazil,
if she looks out the curtained turret
to the street below
and sees us wondering,
driving on.

CENTURY FARM

The green canopy, large umbrella
of the elm on the lawn, its trunk
wider than hay bales and barn doors.
At its foot, a sign:
Century Farm.

Century—where numbers
have been silent before
in notebooks, on chalkboard,
now they jabber and babble—
the dialogue and spin
of zeros makes me really
use the old math—the tree

shrinks to seedling; paved road uncurls
to gravel, red dust. Fence posts
are released from the earth
                    and electricity that makes them hum.
Cars turn to Model Ts, drive right out
of the picture.

To the time before early morning kitchens
came alive with light, before
Arley washed the clothes outdoors—
                                        pale Monday   sunshine,
the wringer washer's churning,
                                        rollers fed a wicker basket heaped
with sheets, towels, their nap
laid flat as they go under.

Plank by square-nailed plank
the walls of the farmhouse
are un-hammered. A team of horses
rides backwards to the sawmill
on the mountain, and mortar
around the fireplace stones
goes soft, spills down the hill
with the tumbling stones
and time.

INVITATION

The invitation of fields, fences,
unlocked doors.

The elegant appeal of columbine,
delphinium, sweet william

at the verandah edge: flowers that summon
hummingbirds in the windless afternoon hush

when parents are napping.
Listen to the evening duty of the dogs

treeing porcupines with an urgent
barking barking.

We just have to look
at what tumbled the garbage pail

on the back step. Switch the outdoor light
for raccoon, wash bear,

made small by being caught.
Invitation: the waterfall at Netty's Turn,

the soft rain and lace
of its falling,

the tide writing runes in the sand
and the names of places, their histories

like the loose bed of rock below
the Landing, rock that once shouldered

a wharf and industry. Old foundation stones
on the Cape invite you to sit

but farmers make sitting
an evening art.

The stones frame a weedy emptiness,
a beckoning.

OLD CABIN RAIN

What we inherit—
the image of our great-grandmother
on her cot reading
holding an umbrella
for the roof leaked in her day too.

And all the pots that Mom can find,
some with bent handles, others
their bottoms black from campfires.
We inherit the sound of rain falling.

The sound of five kids in one bedroom
in sleeping bags, scratch
of horsehair mattresses.
We inherit the rain.

And through dry green curtains
an Irish ploughman sings of his toil,
his song on eight-track tape
leaves the black-topped birch table,
the shelf above the fire,
beach stones and mortar.
The song leaves the machine
turning around on itself,
the ploughman turning adversity . . .

To fall asleep we count
the fireplace stones,
count on the leaking roof, the sound of rain
depending upon kitchen pots,

the ploughman singing to my older blood
turning adversity and damp spirits
to rhyme.

CHARACTERS

1

Nancy's pet raccoon
washed its slender hands

in bowls outside the kitchen step,
inside opened all the cupboard doors

wrack and anarchy: latch them
closed thereafter with elastics

and one night—bump, trickle—
made a waterfall down

the TV's tunnels and tubes—
Coonie banished to the shed.

2

Johnny was the other accident waiting
to count fingers, stitches . . .

spilling kerosene on his shirt.
Check it out: candle on the table, he is

flame, running red and hot in circles
till someone rolls and blankets him.

His cousin. Almost everyone
is somebody's cousin.

3

The farmers have old names
they don't use: Dwight, Irlyn, Forrest.

We call them Skip, Ike, and Tear,
and Mary is matriarch

of the Bigelows, second
mother to my father who summered here.

Maybe now I can . . .
no, can't even chart the long thick

branches of the family trees:
Legge, Lyons, Borden, Bigelow—

they go over the mountain, beyond
the monuments, all through and over

the fields that run to the very edge
of the cliff.

PARTY LINE

A long ring and a short—someone
is calling Theresa down the road.

Two shorts—Connie
as she answers
hears the soft click
of a neighbour listening
from her kitchen.

"Arley, you could ask me
yourself,"
she might say

if she wasn't wondering
what Gloria is cooking
for farmhands
picking apples.

And we keep
to what they hold
dear: secrets are apples
on the tree, there
for the taking, falling
to the ground,
windfall.

SATURDAY NIGHTS

The verandah chairs
we sit on playing cards
and the table are old sage
burlap stretched around
a wooden frame, but the light
through the screen door
is older

than the silhouette of parents inside:
she rises to do dishes,
he places a log on the fire—
that old story of betting on a sure thing.

Another night, restless, we pelt
windfalls from Jim's orchard
at Bible Camp tents.
In the tradition of Lox—
not beaver, badger but shape-changer—
we place molasses, cow skull, & hay
in a sleeping bag. Oh, Lox would laugh
when the campers howled.

But one night we shiver our souls,
transfixed, are thralls
to twilight's diminuendo
as ghost stories escape
from our mouths, of grandmothers
tongue-tied by lightning

as the sky shows her aces:
lights pulse and throb,
Glooscap's practical joke
as if he teaches us a lesson.

THE HOUSE, SO THEY SAY

Who does a farmer call a hippie? Anyone
with long hair, bell-bottoms.
Any youngster they don't know.

It's a woebegone house:
with mossy grey boards
and leaning slightly
in its stillness,
the last house
as you leave Lower Blomidon.

They camp there, live
on sunflowers and no running water
(though I have never seen them).
Summer of low rent and fresh veggies.

Anyone who dares live
in a derelict house.

One night, Kay, Nancy, and I woke
at midnight and swaggered up the road.
We sang, flinging our arms for the rare freedom
of the hour.

Oh, the buzz next morning;
how hippies ran the roads.

SUMMER'S GONE SOUTH

1

In deep snow
an old tractor is covered.
All that shows: trees,
the skeleton of wheels.
There is no end to the field
or sky. All snow,
wheels, branches, twigs,
snow-driven.

2

On the windowsill
the decoy of a duck,
bulrushes in an earthenware pitcher
beside a burlap curtain.
The duck's eye is focused
on a fly in the season's dust.

3

The orchard, rows of trees lost
like a road sacrificing itself
to the horizon,
the vanishing point.
The only hint of harvest,
past and future,
a box bin
waiting for apples.

4

The high tide
is a mirror,
the Cape haunts the Basin:
ghosts of cattle
roam the top of the cliff.

5

The cabin's closed for the winter:
no new entries in the logbook
where we place ourselves
among fields, seasons,
our mythology of Glooscap
who names our lodge.
A fly strip hanging
over the table
is the shape of all our coming and going.

THE BOY WHO FOUGHT WINTER

Nokome, you can't kill
the Ice King, the old enemy
with blizzard hair, crown of icicles,
that awful giant who feasts on the cold

while you watch your people shiver,
huddle around their ornery fires—
they won't burn, wet logs won't dry—

after damp sleep, your hunters
creep out into morning's white offering.
When branches let go snow
and long shadows taunt,
cold breath blows down their necks
and the hunters become the prey
and silent.

No, Nokome, you can't kill Winter.
The bargain Glooscap made
so his people will not succumb
to ease and pleasure all year.

Winter's servants, Frost and Slumber,
could trick you, make you sleep
for six months. I could
stack books and blankets, drift
from January to June
in my warm house

but yours is drafty and the birch bark thin.
Your tall feather comes with effort:
furs, stores of seeds, dried meat,
and branches you strap to your feet
to walk on the white land.

PINK SNOW

Where snow drifts
under Hun's orchard,
December winds carry
the blush of beach and sandstone cliff.

WINTER READING: *BLOMIDON ROSE*

The book opens with travellers
craning their necks for the first glimpse
at the Cape: "beloved landmark,"
North Mountain's abrupt end.

During those slow winters
I read, surveyed the ice, like a hovering osprey,
till it turned March grey
and broke.

                    The book the colour of faded
bee balm, bleeding heart:
I read notes, "returning home,"
in the margins, my father's
underlined phrase, "talk of undercurrents,"
farm kitchen chatter

like the trickle and fall
of stones along the cliff,
"an artist," my great-grandmother,
"found floating on the tide."

As if I'm to crack a code, stones
will break to reveal . . . I split
the book's seams, look for more notes.

I search her painting of the sandstone
walls. Was this the last brushstroke?
She leaned against this length of driftwood
and was lost?

If I could read in the sand
the answer—tide or despair?—

as we praise the colour of her cliffs
—the perfect bloodless red.

BLOMIDON ROSE

AUNT ROSE: I can't for the life think
why anyone would write about me.
I heard the title but did not read the book.
I'm the only Rose
this side of Pereau, unless
the book's about gardens
or the patched flowers
we stitch into quilts?
I was a Green—a green rose—would
the author be mocking that?

RUTH: I am named for that Bible woman
who left her own for her mother-in-law.
"Whither thou goest . . ." we marry our husbands,
their mothers, do what
the farms need; we have to make a living
somehow, and if the book tells her story,
it's our story too.

AUTHOR, ESTHER CLARK WRIGHT: There is no particular
rose; I wrote the "geographical blessing,"
I mention wild as well as
old-fashioned roses growing
in front of white houses, apple blossoms
in "extensive orchards . . . We look
from day to day,
from our homes and homely towns,
across the restless tides . . .

where, to the northward,
Blomidon rises"—

and blooms in our sights,
that wild rose.

"SHE SLEPT OUT"

That July night in '67
when I was nine, the last line
and her nonchalance
when everything was pitched—

the first full summer,
Mom's leisurely descriptions in the log
of trips and hikes, neighbours
over in the evening—
Skip had beer, Arley had tea.

Dad's clipped lines were double-spaced
while the loops and curves of her letters
flowed. She wrote that I slept out.

Pillow on the cot, my sleeping
bag lined from head to toe with cowboys
repeating their lassoes and campfire songs
and yippee-yi-yahs, dust swirling
as they galloped past and circled round,
toe to head, heavy armfuls of rope,
the smell of late evening dew
on the dark,
on the vanishing grass.

THE BIGELOWS' DOG

The first dog of those early
summers, we find him in the photograph
of the apple tree whose low branches
are kindred spirit. He's part
of the story of farms
that offer, casual and reticent,
their produce.
                    Part Everyman's dog,
no particular breed: an agreeable
mix for a farmer's family and chores.

Evening, he saunters up the hill,
assured that Mom will set out
a bowl of scraps: part timekeeper,
quiet eavesdropper, he sits like a pharaoh
on the grass. Later, as darkness
throws out its country-thick blanket,
he'll slip away home.

Part song now with the words "Brownie died,"
of a time when elves left
wet tents on the morning lawn,
when I learned to tie my laces—
wonder of bow and knot—
when one of us slept
on the verandah cot: this luck
smelled of hay, damp grass, and night,
flannel of the inside of sleep.

THE SUMMER OF PIERRE

The summer the baler sliced
the hand of Lou Bigelow's son.
I'm wary of the farm's red machines,
don't want to be ploughed.

He's pale, says Mom of the boy so easy
to ignore. He's been here a week.
He's almost a rumour—so quiet.
Maybe he thinks each English word

will whittle away a finger,
his tongue will go whirligig, dizzying
blur, and fall off. Maybe he thinks if he talks,
English will scratch, bite,

and worse, keep him.
He mopes and sulks.
A word like a barn cat appears,
disappears as quickly as eclipse.

Hard to say what colour it is
and how the word so swiftly finds us.
Homesick, says John who will travel
to Trois-Rivières. Maybe Pierre

pointed to that word. He reads
only half of his book. Maybe
he meant *sickle* for hay field.
The word like tumbling bales.

He's not pleased
to sleep on the verandah cot tonight?
This illness: the dogs have treed a new animal.
Homesick? This place is not a cure?

THE LONG FLOW OF THE MORNING

The nightdress has its day.
7 a.m., at Dan's looking
for an odd job
when she descends to the front step:
his older sister aloof
in a sanctuary of white flannel,
blue flowers

as fresh as if they blossomed
just five minutes ago
in her garden of warm sleep.

She folds the dress around her,
tucks in, and is contained
within its dishabille, her apt
appraisal of the day.

Night's shadows break,
clouds disperse looking
for their lambs and sheep.
Light fastens itself to a fence.

Here there's elbow room,
an elm graces every lawn
and traffic is no more
than one slow tractor.

She wears the long, easy flow
of the morning.

PICKING STRAWBERRIES

For seven cents a box
we wake on a dark summer morning
to porridge the same colour
as fog over the Basin.

In the truck no *hello* or *good morning*:
farmers' words are under their breath,

they plant them
to tease, letting the apple fall
when it's ripe.

Oh, the dry aisles
of pale red soil, strands of straw to say
how they are named, the berries
under the dew-damp cloak.
Hand and wrist go under, are laced
in and wet, are lost—where are they,
the ripe ones?
I find red
and turn it over—to pale green
beads, an empty purse.

They are subterfuge, evasion, seven cents
for how many disguises? Secrets
of algebra—so few notches by my name—
and stifles of geometry: parabola
of my back, grind of knee with sun
breathing down my neck.

Target, aim—
squelch, Nancy's yelp when strawberry
mush stains her.

Lunch break, I lean
into the rocking chair's wicker braid,
listen to father snooze on the cot,
the brook's soft rain.
In the field the women
of Scot's Bay are round, industrious strangers.

FIRST ENTRY

The boys were eleven
in '67 when they took the ladder
at the landing down to the beach,
aiming for that place where rocks
avalanched through the Cape's treed silence
to land with a rock-breaking
thunder on the sand.

A Saturday afternoon when the world was open
and wide as the beach is long.
"We'll walk back to Amethyst Cove,"
says Dougie to the other three.
"I betcha we can find big rocks."

"There's no Amethyst Cove,"
says cousin Kenny.
He rolls his eyes
and Doc, the other local boy,
punches Dougie in the shoulder.

John, the boy from away, the only one
who doesn't know the halfway mark.

Time is a rock they toss
at the cliff, a rock
that lands at their feet.
Life is simple, three-sided:
day, dusk, and night.

They yak about freckles, farts,
knock-knock jokes, wrestling on Saturday night TV
as they walk under the cliff that becomes
an occasional face or animal that roars
inside, captured as it was in stone—
they hear it as a trickle of sandstone
breaking free.

They trust they'd recognize the cove
by some omen or sign
of the land, so they keep walking, keeping
close to the cliff, that soft red wall
that holds the Cape back.

But are so intent on finding
a place they can name Amethyst Cove,
place of doubtlessness,
rumour-come-true.

They are so busy thinking about breaking,
teasing, cajoling rocks to reveal their purple secrets
they don't notice the tide like a scolded boy
who escaped from his room
to find them.

Water like the trickster Lox.

So when they turn back
to see from where they are
halfway—this their measure of the world—
they find the tide close.

No longer discoverers, they are
navigators of the afternoon.

And so wrote John, my brother,
when he was eleven in '67:
"The tide coming in, we got caught coming back.
Dougie—one foot wet, Kenny one foot, Doc both damp,
John both soaked!"

He earned his watermark,
wrote of it, his first entry in the log.

COMMUNITY PICNIC, AT THE LOOKOFF

After the eating, the pony rides
and baseball game, we were
still restless and roaming
so we wandered through the gift shop
inspecting polished amethyst

before we made our way
up the tower of white painted stairs,
to the fourth floor landing where
we signed the guest book
        Mickey Mouse
        Elvis
        Mary Poppins
thinking that was the greatest joke.

We climbed more white stairs. They grew
steep and we probably slowed down,
especially when adult legs
descended, weaving past our hive
of apprehensions, stifled laughs.

Finally we climbed into air,
the railed square where we looked down
at the field where women
packed leftover food and lawn chairs,
the men taking in
the ease of one Sunday off
and grandparents taking quiet inventory of who was
and wasn't there last year.

We might have seen this
through the trees. They might have been elms
sixty feet tall and we were above them,
thinking this as we turned, looked,
and gasped at the world below:
a truck smaller than a toy
turning that sharp 90 degrees by the Pereau
church, the sweep of summer-long fields,
the amplifying silence.

GAMES

Hiding behind hay bales,
box bins, tractors, corner
of the bunkhouse: hide-
and-seek at Ike's with someone
at the big elm, the slur of numbers
running to rhyme, counting,
counting on the perimeters,
the periphery of twilight.

In the fall, middle
of the road: the hockey puck
slammed, flies into potato fields—
the game stops
when the one car that day
is patient. Nets are portable

until the orchard or beach
or the frogs in Bert's pond
catch the boys' attention.
They swirl their towels, whip
like swords, the loose ends:
we shriek, run in circles—

play crib in a tent-trailer
on Johnny's lawn. Murky light
through green canvas, the radio plays
"The Lion Sleeps Tonight."
I like the part where the voice warbles,
roars like a young cub learning,
on a hill high above grass lands,
satisfied by his accomplishment,

as we score and follow
the journey our pegs make
around the board.

PAGEANTRY: THE RED BARN

We meander home past midnight
in darkness that has us
tentative, keyed

to every vigilant sound. Later
we'll listen: where the pulsing
hum of electric fence ends

driveway begins.
But the Red Barn in the gully,
its rumours of haunted, like straw
under our shirts: itch
so we inch open the wide
barn doors, huddle
around hay bales when Johnny says, "Three knocks
mean the dead want to talk."

And of course we hear two solid knocks,
listen for the third, to the dark
dry silence as if the dead have lost their stamina,

are hesitant and want us
to wait, want us listening, our full
white-knuckled attention, complete immodesty—

the lightning of the third knock.
Nancy keels over, lies there
while we squint

and gauge her inky
silhouette. And every time we walk past the Red Barn again
we hasten our step, listen.

THREE QUEENS, FIVE JOKERS

The pack of cards is the first thing
we throw in the bag: Gin

Rummy, Crazy
Eights, Crib, Forty-fives at the Red Camp.

We pack bacon, beans, watermelon—
don't care about travelling light

since we know the road:
take a left, cross the Borden Brook, keep

left at the fork—there
we'll see the camp if night

isn't as dark as mink.
Kerosene; dark corners

are silent, damp. Johnny unpacks the cards,
coy smile, says, strip poker?

We regroup, fidget,
raise eyebrows; whispers, subtle smiles.

No is the wild card we throw out
and *yes* is adult, sweet challenge.

We'll call your bluff
and dare and hold our cards

close to every button, zipper, belt,
and knot. We're outnumbered: three queens

to those jokers. *We're not gonna*
show you nothing.

NANCY'S WATERMELON

Night at the Red Camp,
we slap cards down,
flippant remarks about her stacked deck.
She doesn't know our teasing
is just a cow chewing its cud, round
and endless round.

And without a word—
gone. She found her way out
and down, over tree roots, branches

silently, darkly wrapping
the path, muscle and teeth
where they weren't
before. Her heart would be ruffed
grouse beating its wings. She'd shift
in her pack the awkward weight

that she later threw down
at the Cookhouse Turn.

Next morning
10 a.m. sun drying
the slurry of pink flesh on pavement,
slippery black seeds like pennies
we counted to up the ante

and oh, the pale
green and white cracked smile.

BEACH NOTES

1

Over electric fences,
outskirt of pasture, long grass,
through aisles of orchard where tractors
score the earth

then down the cliff by ladder
or—if it's broken by weather—we go
where the orchard slopes
into stepping stones in the creek
(pronounced *crek*).

We dive off the House-Rock
into cold—shrinks your hale soul—
cold water, swim to what high tide
leaves: torn blanket of sand

as *warm* and *sun*
swim back to us.

2

The Slippery Rock, named
for green algae threads
that when smooth and wet
make our waterslide,

our summer skating rink:
ebb tide, mudflats: rich red sand
oozes up between our toes.
We paint red mud gloves
on our arms, wash off
in the distances of Minas Basin.

3

Beach-trek to Nancy's
if tide cooperates . . .
but it captures us
out on a point—avalanche
of other years, where,
caterpillar to sequoia, we try
to scale the cliff:

red sand under our clawing fingernails.

4

Once on a summer's night
where sandpipers by day
skirt and tally the water's edge,
we fill pockets with Fundy kelp,
                    dulse
                                  lay it on the lawn to dry

and later chew
its salty purple leather,
spit it out.

5

Check the trawls
—baited hooks on a weighted
plank—we catch a wormy
tommy cod.

Mr. & Mrs. Camera
ask us to hold it up
as if it's an oyster
or pearl—*click*
—for a dime.

INDIAN PAINTBRUSH

We can't help
ourselves—the slope,
the tall grass, us
rolling through it, tumbling, falling
as the field murmurs
                lie down
and *cover me*—
the field a canvas.

Lie down   *cover me*—
the flowers paint us.

THE TIGHT WEAVE

Throw open the root cellar's
angled doors—you'll hear
the scratch of claw; scrawny cat
peers from musty corners
into daylight where we set up
tent on Nancy's lawn.

The lawn that drops
to cliff, beach, the slow
erosion of tide

though we're preoccupied with things
growing: apples, strawberries, fields of hay
we are careful to walk around.

We're careful with the cats too
who are wild, who skirt sunlight,
bales of hay in the Old Barn
where we climb and swing on ropes.

We try to count and pat the cats
after Nancy says kittens were born last week.
The mother in search of food ventures out,
then wails and runs away.

I look out at the tide
growing watery red
over the maroon mud flats.

Throw open—no, close the cellar doors,
don't let him . . .

I don't hear them closing,
though the thud and scratch
in my throat, the hollow in my gut
doesn't go away.

There's the banshee wailing and pleading,
the hollow heavy sound when it sinks in:
drawstring bag,
the unusual tight weave of burlap.

DESSERTS

The corner store comes to Nancy's door—
the yellow grocery truck, promise
of the delicious week come true.
While Arley and Aunt Rose buy practical
milk and bread, we bring
bottles we trade—tinkle, clink . . .

                                        . . . the grocer snaps
brown paper wings with one hand,
they become bags he fills
as we—
                three, four, five fireballs, sourballs!—
count caramels, jawbreakers, flying saucers,
gold coins and kisses,
angel mints, cracker jacks
with whistle prizes and sweet tart
necklaces we bite off the string
one at a sugary and sour time.
We snuffle powdery grains
of filled straws when we sneak
down to the wide red ribbon
of the beach

and strawberries straight from the field
will be shortcake tonight
after I help hull the berries—
syrupy red stain and juice
on fingers, leafy hats
drop into the grainy slats
of boxes—scarlet beads and the day
topped with cream.

BY THE BIGELOWS' BARN

Barn swallows fly and dart
to rafters where they nest.
Their sharp anthem, arabesque.
We swing on pulley ropes
thinking they're meant for us:
farm work, our easy labour.

Dusk, in the hayfield we lie
on our stomachs on the trailer,
tractor-pulled. The farmer throws bales
like a child playing with coloured blocks
while we trail our fingers
through the tickling grass.

But the cow paddy
by the barn—I thought
old and baked:

one white sneaker

now is wet and brown,
shame's sullen colour.

I leave it
to dry by Arley's wood stove, learn
how to walk again, barefoot
where the hay is cut
short and sharp.

AWAKENING, CAMPING TRIP

Dad packs food, tarp, and axe,
the billy can for tea,
then the boys pose under
the apple tree. Knapsacks,
full for one night, round their shoulders
as if they venture
into the deepest,
darkest continent.

"Throw out your jokers," Dad says,
handing Ian the cards.
When, lighter, they set out,
we, the sisters left behind,
are boats at Pereau wharf
leaning at low tide.

Boats stranded
by the lowest tide.

Why couldn't we . . . ?

The question winds around
the winding mountain road
but it can't find them.

At camp, the boys build a ring
of stones, a fire. They tally the rabbits,
grouse, and squirrels seen.

Next morning when they wake
a doe softly on cloven hoof
will have a long look
at them, a good long look
at their silence.

MOUNTAIN WALK

Walking through fields
she tells me ghost stories.
I clutch her hand.
She breathes
mist, says *evening*
as the fields darken

says *night*,
haunting
as a breeze shivers
over tall grass,
as mist now
grows out of every rock.

HALLOWEEN ON THE CAPE

The night always darker
than bulrushes kerosene-soaked
for weeks—oh, we made plans—
The night lit with sparklers,
firecrackers, the voices
from nowhere of older brothers
who play the trickster.

And the bale of hay where the path
goes up the mountain—it too
wants to light the night.
Flames grow tall as cornstalks
and taller again over party lines. Danny's
                    our eavesdropper—he's breathless
and huffing:
                         "They said . . . hippies
setting fires
and your Mom said . . ."

                                             Tumult and clash,
stomping of boots and ash, we throttle,
                    race through the woods, the thick brush
as flames and words chase us:
they are a moose, anarchy
of its crashing limbs.

When we find the night again
we pledge secrecy—tree stump
as bible, no word
about tonight.

No word
but the flag we raise:
painted skull and crossbones—
at the Bible camp. It flew
for several quiet weeks
until Aunt Rose took it down.

DON FORSYTHE'S STORE

It was called *Forsythe's*
or *Don's* after the man
who tallies on paper, long hand
what we owe him.

On packages of cigarettes,
in the margins of old newspapers,
the figures. He crouches over the counter
adding the cost of milk, ice cream for the five of us.

> *Oh, some bacon too,*
> *and eggs.*

Don carries the figures faster than
I can take it in—the stuff for sale
here in the store centred around a wood stove.
Everything: shelves full of cans, boxes
and cogs, blades and boots: some even
hang from the ceiling.

He is stocked for the generations
of a farm—they all come to the store,
young and old and in-between,
though Don says under fifty
you're a youngster.

The old men always
play cards, stoke the fire,
put fuel on the fire of wisecracks.

Entering the store
we interrupt their repertoire
and mumbled chat. I can never
quite catch their laid-back drift
or look them fully in the face,
more interested in how Don reaches
for the top shelf with a rake-like instrument.

Or maybe I'm shy, don't like how the men
turn from their talk to see exactly
who rings the bell above the door.

"Oh, you're Dave's daughter," they say
when I offer my full name. To strangers
we are always our father's child

as if we're caught in the time before we came:
how long it had been there—the yellow strip
of tacky paper that whorled and caught
an archaeology of flies.

Outside the fields are flat
to the edge of the cliff. We look out
at Paddy's Island with its sandstone arch
that will disappear, as the island too,
over time, will disappear.

THE NEW COTTAGE

MOVING DAY

Ian, always climbing, always falling,
topples out of an apple tree.
We are moving today: he drops
out of our nest.

Somebody's borrowed truck—
we've packed all the old dishes,
the binoculars, the plaster angel
over the fireplace, my great-grandmother's
painting of the beach.

We moved horsehair mattresses,
the table with birch bark legs,
have picked the last of the wild berries
that are smaller, sweeter than
those in Woolaver's field.
We put our berries in boxes stained
with strawberries of other years.

We leave where Grammie Saunders
slept. We walk through the cabin one last time
asking her ghost to join us at the new lodge.
Our words echo in empty rooms
and we fall away.

GLOOSCAP'S LODGE: A HOUSEWARMING

An emptiness: the old camp's fireplace
bulldozed over the hill, road paved over the living
room. Tires sigh
to Glooscap's ghost in the birches.

But rafters and new walls grow,
tucked behind Ike's pasture,
heaven's hill up the road,
North Mountain.

My father drives nails,
sweats drops as round as nail heads.
The carpenter sneaker-prints
lumber that later climbs the A-frame
as if
                —agile, agile—
he can walk on walls.

This world smells of sawdust, pine,
lime juice Mom brings with cookies
in the afternoon: from chartreuse bottle
syrup is mixed with sugar, mountain-soft water.

We dangle our legs from the upstairs loft,
listen to the knot of saw,
sawing of wood, percussion of hammer,
shingles and cedar shakes.

On the verandah wall under
antlers, they sign their names—
now ingrained—neighbours
who christen Glooscap's Lodge,
the reach of its A-frame slope.

LOFT

God's eye is orange, red, and green,
loose ends of wool wrapped
around two sticks hanging
under the upstairs sloping roof.

A window and hook
latch onto another smaller eye.
Look down at woodpile, back step,
tree-covered hills climbing into mountain.

On a shelf—bright cats' eye marbles
and dinky toy dump trucks
parked in the dust of
when we plowed them through gravel.

Loft: where a friend visiting
sleeps tight under the eaves. She'll wake
flustered, breathless, with a wooden nightmare
she bumped her head on,
a dream that wants to press its sharp angles.
It's snug, Linda, only snug.

Loft: room to where warm air rises,
room that ends like a shelf. Peek
downstairs at socks drying
on the wagon wheel hanging
over the fireplace.

A-frame loft: made from the *A*
in abide, ascend, arrow to the sky,
room where you can hear
raindrops when they break abundantly
on the peak of our lodge, our reservoir.

HEIRLOOMS

The black-topped table
with legs of birch trees bent
in the 1920s or before—
we know to hold our cards
and pull them flat
off the table's ragged edge. Bid
thirty for sixty if you have the ace
of hearts and jack

because I have the five
but if we're two, we'll play Crazy
Eights, Fish, Old Maid—
me in Harry's chair, named
for its previous owner: round arms
slouch into sagging seat—perfect
to watch the fire feed
on its hot geometry.

And you in the wicker rocker—
smooth curve of its back,
its arms unraveling
to my great-grandmother
painting, blending
red ochre, burnt umber
for the colour of the cliffs.

And my mother will choose paint for the wooden
rocker: red for Grammie Saunders,
red clover, raspberries, red-letter
days all summer, the fire

with its tunnel to the roof,
for strawberries hulled in the sun.
She paints the chair sweet, paints
her cradle red: she'll afternoon nap
in the chair that moves
toward the very earth.

COTTAGE OWLS

To the Great Gray,
the Long-eared, the Eastern Screech,
Great Horned, the Snowy, Spotted,
the Short-eared, the Elf,
the Flammulated—

add to these the owls we collect:
the Embroidered Pink,
Mexican Papier-Maché,
Macramé Jute, Bronze Wind Chime,
the Shaking Bobble Head,
and the Salt and Pepper Owls.

(I thought Isle Haute in the bay
was named for the owls' call.)

Length: 3–7 in.
What to Look for: hand-stitched feathers,
stoic plastic, knots for
interrogating eyes.

Habitat: any upper shelves,
indiscriminate wall
or thin branch the wind tips
as if the owls will say
why they are so aloof.

Migration route: random,
spontaneous, highly
debatable—we can't say from whom
or where they so quietly came.

Known for: inactive, sleepy days
though at night they stir
in the fire-shadows,
feed foremost on whispers, sleepover
of twelve kids in the loft:

wink, wink, coven of smirk, hiccup,
stifled laugh, farce
of *dormez-vous*.

AFTER THE CHORES

When the hills of North Mountain lean,
when wood splitting turns
to a solid stacked cord and lemonade,
when the verandah's view is too many
saplings, spruce trees, the valley green—
we're in the hollow behind cow pasture
and the Red Barn—
when he's drawn a line
of plumbing, dug in
to bring soft water to our sink,
when the nap is over and
late afternoon claims the sun,
when the five of us and farmers
nearby are too large a family
since he grew up with Skip and Bouk and Hun:
his summer brothers, the way
some places have summer kitchens,
when milk and butter cool in the brook,
when it's too much—
he's hemmed in, the cabin tucked into the hillside,
the orchard's green haze, when hills
and slopes are not shelter, but arms too tight—

it's my father's time
to climb the hill above the orchard
and find fields that lay themselves out,
run flat out to the edge of the cliff
and sometimes fall
to the beach below—

trees lose horizon,

cows think
the earth abruptly ends.

He sits silent at the hilltop.
It's my father's time.

MILK AGATE

The summer-long beach
and those stones:
flint, amethyst, milk agate.

Stones that are themselves
the hours rock hunting on the beach,
hours with your head down
as you walk slowly
or crouch down, dreaming
the promises in stone.

Flint: you want Indian campfires,
arrowheads, something smooth you can hold
in your hand, something that sparks
legend and quartz-white lies
father told of wigwams.

Amethyst: in our spring, fall, and winter house
our wish stone on the mantel
between a green sea urchin
and the clock, reminder of Amethyst Cove
that can't be found, where this stone
like dandelions grows rampant
and wild.

Milk agate: pieces of foggy dreams,
currents that take you out to sea,
beyond . . . you are lost
for graceful hours on the sand
with the red cliff

breaking off and falling . . .
a crop of rocks
at its base.

Here you can find
shards of history, seascapes,
the colours of paintings by Turner,
foggy and obscure abstracts,
chaotic storms and shipwrecks,
landscapes of a lost relative:
in the cloudy cream of milk agate
you can begin to see
how an artist here
could have drowned.

TRANSLATIONS FROM THE LOG

Ian needs his "ears lowered"—
someone to cut the brown fringe
above them so we can see
his freckles as round as the heads of nails
in barn board.

"Chewed" is what farmers do
in the off hours, Bouk or Tear
or Skip, what you try to make
sense of—sound like tobacco.
They roll it; it thickens inside
till the mumbling is
a brief story, understated.

"Puttered," the engine that could,
of her, author of the every
day, the usual, the occasional "ugh"
(a bat) or sudden whack,
a bird slams the window.
The days like this, like feathers:
some brown, the others
violet, emerald.

And "everyone drifted"
means the five of us somewhere
between Nancy's—end of the road—
or up the mountain, down
the beach or roaming
any nearby town: Canning, Kentville,
New Minas.

At day's end
my mother's last sentence tallies
who's where; sometimes
home has us "all
to bed."

NOT MOTHER, MAY I

Not *Red Rover, Red Rover, let Nancy come over*,
not two lines of kids in the schoolyard,
or I Spy or Mother, May I—

Not *may we . . .* ? Few questions—
they are the calf that wandered off,
but "we're staying at Nancy's."
Mom nods, sure and yes,
when we don't ask, when we're in Johnny's tent—
Coonie in the shed, or at the Red Camp
or when we swim for the third time today—we may

or may not, given when the tide's high:
multiply any number by countless possibilities
beginning with cape, beach, cards
after corn boil, bonfire, trawls to tend,
and hide-n-go-seek at Ike's.

Worry is not in her log entries,
not in her lexicon of Blomidon
where we know every farm dog
and all the family names.
Worry is a city cousin, far away.

She's not concerned about midnight's
"hippie" stroll, fireworks all those raucous
Halloweens anywhere between Pereau
and the dark shoulder of the Cape, dark night
lit with a magician's wand and plumes.

Most evenings end
with her words in the log
of “kids all over” at different houses, camps, and tents—
up and down the road.

CARD PARTY, WHITE WATER'S HALL

Bouk, my first partner, nods
so briefly I can't tell if it's hello
or play a good game.

At home, he doesn't talk
when we gather, Saturday night,
to watch The Hulk sling Good Guy Googan
over his shoulder: after the match
they muckrake and roar, blood
vessels bursting.

Skip shuffles the pack:
muffled words slip
between the cards he deals
with a sure hand. I'm sure
I'll fumble and lose decorum and game.
We wait as Bouk arranges his cards, bids,
and leads with a ten, pulling trump—we take
the trick

and the second too.
Changing tables,
he says, "Not a bad hand"
in his discouraged

exuberance. Should I nod? Put on
a poker face?
                    I'm the queen
of no trump, can't tell what is up
or down, spades or hearts, where

my body ends and heads prevail,
as if reason should?

Oh, intermission means
cards turn into cakes and tarts—
and the game is sweet.

THE STORY

The question of rum missing from the top shelf
where he kept precisely five bottles—remember
those open shelves in front of
a mirror from the old camp?
What's the story
or the question of the story? The rum
and cider they brewed all year:

Oh, a good year, vintage
the best year, but too wet
for cabbage and berries,
a good year for rum.

They drank how much cider at Bouk's
that winter's night, the harvest wrapped up
months ago? How much did they make?
The first time I thought about a farmer's
wage, I searched for the key in Marion's kitchen.
Where did they hide it? Like looking
for a living from the land. I was almost locked out.

Was it a question of farmers on winter nights?
All that . . . *physicality*
locked in. Or was it the slow taste
of regret? Did they sip on that or toss it back
and move on? Who was the rascal
who suggested they move on,
see what Dave had on his top shelf?
Was the cottage door open or did Hun
have the key? Was it impulse?

Or a curiosity, an empty cottage?
How often did they nip in—
a conspiracy of farmers
watering down the drink? They took
only a dram, expected
my father to not notice?
Did they glimpse the collected owls?

They keep silent
witness. What about Erlyn in
and they "had a few" the week before?
Or my father was an owl after a mouse?
Was it a question of cider and rum
or the story of one owl.

BLOMIDON DOGS

The dogs stand guard
at the foot of driveways,
their pink, spoon-shaped tongues
hanging out, keen eyes alert.
They're eager to corral the cattle.

Start at Bigelows', end of the road
where everyone can name
the dog and its predecessors.
Each farm has a genealogy
of animals related, by blood
and temperament, story
or preference—raccoon, porcupine.

The dogs are constant, dependable
though the farmers wince slightly,
remembering the ones too quick
or dull.

A farm with no dog
is a house without a tall elm,
a barn without hay
and swallows who dart between the rafters.

When the dogs bark at night, we know
which one sits at the foot of a random tree.
The dogs do their chores
while the cows are islands
we cannot find in the dark night field.

CLOTHES FOR BLOMIDON

Stanfield's woollen socks
fill black gumboots topped
with red stripe: I spread my feet,
feel like a farmer tractoring along a field,
through orchard, pulling potato bags,
stacking flats of berries, shaping
a living from that.

I gather wood
for fire that warms damp wood-stove nights.
Lucky me to touch wood, kindling.

A chalky white sweater,
tall to the neck and thigh, keeps wind
from navigating land and sea charts
of marrow, bone. Blow me down
or keep me standing with the wind.

And if it's colder I'll borrow
Dad's black and red plaid jacket
from the hook above the cot.
What I wear here:

weathers puddles of driveway mud,
damp pastures, tasks of gathering—
buckets from the brook,
blankets that go back
to my great-grandparents—
I clothe myself in fire,
earth, air, and florid water.

NEW CABIN VISITORS

Cows on the verandah:
a mother and calf stare
through the front window,
and hummingbirds fly to
that soft violet stalk: delphinium.

Other visitors, blatantly
invited, hike to Cape Split where the dog
corners a porcupine
and the world ends
in wind, tall November grass.

After cross-country skiing, the cabin's
armchairs are full of us,
tired by the well-tended fire.
Empty bowls of chili on the table;
easy dishes cooked in the largest pot.
We traipse buckets
from the brook, slop mountain
cold water on linoleum.

They write in the log,
sign it so we know whose
loops, crossed t's, and slant:
the sprawling stretch of superlatives,
the beer between the words
and the *oh, I'll-be-back-soon*
lament.

THE VISITING DOG

Not a gatekeeper, she's a lap warmer
until she squirms and won't fit.
Her head perches hopeful
on Christine's knee; she's devout
or simply wants food
and now curls up by the fire
where we sit with coffees
in the old chairs.

Generous morning wanders
into afternoon—time
for beer, before yes, we should,
we really intend to, and push
ourselves toward the W-word.
She's at the door as we don
jackets, lace boots. She saunters

down the driveway,
sniffs at grass, cow patties
in the pasture, then catches a whiff
of _________? dashes to the barn
where—high-pitched yelp—

                                        she limps
to the cabin where we soothe
her with finger-licks (soft tongue!)
of Rémy Martin, wrestle
quills from her nose, brace her slippery tail
between sliding glass door and any sloping
solid truss that might or could

hold her; she roams,
climbs halfway up the staircase,
searching for the place
with no sharp ends.

A-FRAME CHRISTMAS

We wanted nothing
of our summers to change, everything
to last and last longer: long entries in the log,
many sketches, maps of we hiked that far,
caught so many—

Card parties, Valentine
suppers at the hall where women
stitched quilted flowers and squares
and farmers wore long sleeves.

All year Christmas was a question and talk,
a dream of a tree somewhere tucked
under our long A—

We'd hang wet socks on the wagon wheel,
tinsel from antlers.

Talk, a jewelled bird
perched on a branch.

Talk, all the other birds
can fly. Dad mutters
"too much at home"—
the weight of five sighs:
from a tree somewhere
glass balls and icicles fall.

And slowly as years pass
we name the new ornaments:
apples all year in the orchard.

STRANDED

Rumour is a farmer
who throws the crop
over the cliff with the cow.

It's no slow tractor,
not a bicycle or the wind
that carries the tide in
and news of missing persons.

We make our way
to the end of the road
where trucks are parked
at the bottom of the Cape draped
in summer fog. The fog that bit off
more than the rain
and headland of Blomidon.

Rumour at the end of the road, its tether
is rubber boots, the trek up the mountain,
the search on the beach.
It's the rocks of the old wharf
and no wood left.

It's farmers talking low
of strategy. They fill their boots
with dense muscles as they knead
and shuffle, as the heavy tires of their trucks
stand on paved earth.

It’s men going off
to find the missing, to revive rumour
that, this time, will be
the anonymous mother and child
found hugging the sandstone cliff.

FROM LOG ENTRIES, JUNE '86

: wading in the tide.
I disturb a promenade of gulls—
prance, jig, and liftoff:
choreography on the sand.

: went out to the road
to talk to the cows:
they keep conversation
in their bald eyes, expect
translation, and stare.

: up through the night
to flashes of lightning,
rain on the roof's
rain-splitting peak.

: morning sky clearing, everything,
all the leaves and trees
a darker shade green,
chlorophyll's blush.

THE LAST ENTRY

The reluctance in the last entry:
to leave without a hope,
a wish, a next time we'll do this,
a promise and tidy cabin

to walk up the Cape,
slip through the trees,
listen to the lace of the falls.

To open the door for Ben the cat
and stroke him, setting off
his motor.

Hope's threads in the air
or is that morning fog?
The reluctance to wake too soon.
Instead we lounge, let the fire catch kindling
that drops from the trees on the hillside,
while we brew a big breakfast
and quietly write in the log—
forgot last night.

Oh, if blossoms, potatoes, and berries
wait, remain elusive
until we return
a harvest that procrastinates
for our promises—

Summer doesn't start till we arrive,
calendar pages in farm kitchens

set alight in the stove. We keep
our agreement with the seasons:
spring's road hockey,
summer's hide-n-go-seek—

In the seeker's rhyme at the tree
can you hear Glooscap's song
to turn Summer's head, come north?

BLOMIDON NIGHTS

1

We travel the road
in the dark that arrives
like a deer in headlights

sit in the centre
of the road, tell ghost stories,
sing ballads,
ignoring the cars
—if any—that move around us.

We go down to the beach,
hold onto roots and weeds
on the polished path.

Evening, we are the locals
out on the road between apple trees,
barns, and the Bay of Fundy.
We move with the tide
and seasons and night.

2

Come back in ten years.
The road is empty now;
its path has changed.
They've built picnic tables
and a bridge over the falls.

Our echoes are in apples.
Our echoes are in apples.

THE CORE TO KEEP

The field where grass grows tall
through a harrow's rusty spokes,
cultivated in 1945, was home
to Newton, Henderson, Josh Porter.
Now spruce trees
border picnic tables, and tents
that come October will harvest a silence
that settles under the old foundations.

Someone's built new bungalows
but reliable rumour says another old-timer
is sick, has died—demise
of the small farm. When
did they plough down the orchard?

The young and middle-aged
have moved on, the party lines
gone: we can't eavesdrop
on talk like that brook in summer that dries up.
Words to farmers are the core
of apples they throw away.

•

I've slept, it seems, for twenty years,
walk out this afternoon
to the tide coming in with the same
patience and draw, the cliffs
the same strange blush and rouge
just as my great-grandmother painted them—

the earth, at least, keeps
its old perfections.

A GIFT OF CHERRIES

As everything is
around a time and place
and is not . . . I'm suddenly transported
by taste:

Bill pedals, we go double
all the way up the road,
up hills and down,
all for the cherry trees
at Harry Woolaver's farm.
We whiz by farmhouses,
roadside elms, slow down as we climb hills.

As everything is,
it so quickly loses its place, memory's valley,
. . . scrunch of bicycle wheels in the courtyard
surrounded by house, barn,

and four trees,
an open space, enclosed, carpeted
with the sound of beige stones,
the air dusty with
should-we-be-here-do-we
have-to-be-secret?

As everything is,
its magic elusive or dreamt,
dismounting, you can't even put your foot down
to touch it—I flew
or floated or dreamt myself

into the easy-to-climb branches
of one of Harry's famous, but short-lived,
what-became-of-his-oh-his-beautiful
cherry trees?

To this day
I can taste their concealment.

NORTH MOUNTAIN FIX

On top of the Cape,
old foundation stones are overcome
by grass—where are the Indian
Paintbrush, those red flames in the fields?

Hay mounds loose and itching
to be elsewhere—all winter
I want to be elsewhere—
there where ghosts in the trees
walk out and tell stories.

Where twilight called us
to hide and one to seek,
heard us counting at the largest elm—
her eyes closed, slurring
the number rhyme
while the rest scattered.

I'm drawn to that tree
as if, in a previous life,
it was a shaman.

I need my North Mountain fix,
meandering balm of the red sand beach,
mudflats' slip and blue sheen
and the tide to reach.

I need the noble slope
of the Cape. Everything in flux
and transient in me

needs its stability:
the cliffs are drawbridge,
fortress walls, and anchor.

EVERY ELM AND STORY

Driving slowly past the inns
and stately homes of Wolfville
with their turrets and widow's walks:

    on the rooftop I pace
    as I bide my time, a nineteenth century
    storm, my husband out to sea—

At the farm market: box bins
full of the tang
of apples, the dusty smell of potatoes
with earth still on them.

And crossing the Acadian dyke, I almost
see boats departing. Clutching
their prized pottery, did they scan
the fields, survey hard work
and sigh, as they coaxed the children
and marched along?

In Canning a stump of the old elms
says   *time is getting old,*
says   *romance has folded up its green tent.*

The August sun on hay bales as round
and full as old skirts, as fields
that want to touch water—they reach
to the edge of the cliff.

And then every house:
each one with many names and a chapter.

To the top of the Cape, I drive
through what was once the living
room of the old cabin
as if I'm running over the old stories,
and new ones too. The road
loops around them both.

We spread out salads,
scan the wide field and water
so far,
so quietly below.

What everything tells me.
My task: to write the long,
last entry in the log.

GLOOSCAP'S FIRE

On the beach, late afternoon,
lying under a June sun relearning
its warmth. I sit up, woozy
at the expanse: water,
sea-acres away
beyond terracotta sand.

I turn to the Cape's solid presence
—it will steady me—
expecting Glooscap,
good and powerful Chief,
to stroll out, silent,
surveying the land and seascape.

My father, home from those hills
said he saw the ring of Glooscap's tent,
stirred the fire's embers.
We fell asleep to stories
of Summer winding a goldenrod trail,
dropping petals of brown-eyed Susans
as she drifted south after her six months;
stories of stones he hurled
into the bay. We know them
as cousins:
                    Five Islands.

Kespeadooksit, "*the story ends*"
I think   good night, good sleep.
Kind neighbour, grandfather,
thank you for the stories,
this place. Good sleep.

ARCHIVES

PHOTOGRAPH WITH DUTCH DOOR OPEN

That's when I stop—
somewhere a tractor sputters.
Turn the key—thump and the engine
drums again—

particular morning after
a fishing or hunting party
as early as 1920 or the war years:
which generation, father or grandfather,
left his wet boots to dry beside
the fireplace in black and white?
There's no date on sunlight

like stage lighting
that bleaches chunky beach stones,
over-exposure melts the mortar,
tightens its grasp on a tall walking stick
leaning like a gun.

The sun wants to go hunting?

Or to take that stick
in its big white hands and stir
the coals and sparks to flame?

Still life, mantel: dark bottles of ale
I can't read or date, shadowy margins;
two with candles frame a set
of antlers, five points that won't stop—
flash of white tail—or run.

We lost the huntsmen—
no captions or names, no fish
in the shallow pan—we must make our clues
from those drying boots, one lace
reaching to an old hooked rug,
from the deep pot pulled away by cast iron
arm, the charred, notched,
and sunlit edge of the surviving log,
post-mortem—soft grey dune,
erosion of ash

which will claim dry wood,
the camera-shy table and chair,
the story I've been looking for:
cabin as pushed, hunted
and burnt unseen
that now I mourn.

GREAT-GRANDPARENTS SAUNDERS

There's no logbook for the day
he left the pie social, White Water's Hall
when the sudden aphasia
of the mind, soundless
clamour, chaos, acute
chest pain as if the Ice King
struck him with a dagger
of frost.

His widow's silence deeper than black
and white photographs,
the sound of her quiet strokes
of paint, the diary where she hid
her grief, pentimento,
repentant, a painted landscape
that she paints over
until she went down
to the beach
one morning—

WHARF

The darkest part of the photograph
—swart, swagger, obscuring char
of tide, Fundy's ink has drawn
its shadows on the stones: anchor
and bed for the logs
arranged on that thin peninsula:

hwearf. Can you hear the old-world
heave, the ox pull of trees felled
and milled, the clang of mallet
against spike and steel? Echo

of promontory—you start to say
promise and those sounds leak,
slope into water, those three tiers:

the first closest to the cliff and falls
—thread of white water, end
of the Borden Brook.
Nine stacked logs hold
the grassy point that plunged—
thunder of hooves, shotgun
of earth slap.
                    A few yards out,
five logs high, beginning of
diminuendo, waste-me-away, water

reclaiming
the surviving posts
in the last

brief mound of rock.

THINK EVENING

On the verandah steps she sits
facing west, looks away
from the photographer
as if grief is a seed that grows
a tall weed if she meets his gaze.

Here where delphinium
petals are crumpled notes, a letter
she wants to write: "mother . . .
passed away . . ." but the words
won't do. They float and drift.

Strolling on the beach, does she
begrudge water's rumoured pull?
Can she swim without questions?

She paints flowers,
paints light on black basket and trays.
Isn't summer's sadness the worst?

Have her eyes always been downcast?
The silence around her mother's death—
it swells and ebbs, Fundy's abundance
and low points.

Think evening, going all the way
out to the mud flats, coming home
with nothing, not even
one pocket of dulse.

THE YEARS MAPPED OUT

Circa 1890, the Bordens milled,
sluiced logs down the brook.
My father's drawn it like railroad tracks
with arrows—go this way, spring
runoff: roar, scrape, and grind,
the forest's teeth bite into that deluge
of dark juice, sludge, and mire before
the lumber floats, purrs
and gurgles, goes mute
and is shipped out.

He's mapped the family too:
Sir Frederick and Lady B. outlived
their son killed in the Boer War
and daughter lost at sea.

After the *fin de siècle*, world weariness
consumed like caviar? Horses and tight chains
dragged logs to the edge, fifty foot drop—roil
and crack. The boom below: premonition
and echo of Europe's Great War.

Timber, dominoes go down:
Christmas 1939, he's ten
at the end of the road. Wet snow
melts where he walks.

Here we might mark an *X*—
a seed falls, a path opens—that day
he studied the white breath

and muscled strain: eight teams
of horse and oxen hauling a black
metal animal—a boiler—
up the mountain road.

They'll build a fire under its belly
so it will steam, work
the steady chug of its arm at the mill.
They'll move it five times
before the big forests disappear.

Here I might cut another *X* in hardwood
if I could find some. Instead I'll circle
—think of trees he will later cultivate
and tree rings, no beginning or end—
the day he decided his career.

HAYING, 1941

I

A hay field, cut short, the slope
like a dog leaning into a scritch.
Someone's tractor tires
have flattened a path;
Bill has driven into the next scene, offstage.
It's July or August, unusual
that wind has gone
AWOL:
what is cut away, diminished return.

II

The driver of the truck in shadow,
someone else with pitchfork
tosses loose hay
into exuberant excess.
An owl,
a wingèd beastie in the pile
ready to pounce.

III

Sunday, they pose beside the lilac—
farmers in jackets or their sons, arms
around each other, though the one in uniform—
if he signed up, did he
come back?

IV

Sickle, blade, scythe,
and haywire—who sleeps
under the haystack?

The boy here is beside
tall grass, lupins, goldenrod,
near a barn's mortar and stone
foundation.
It will be gone
long before the boy's a man.

He has a sulk upon him
and he won't say why.

AT JORDAN RIVER, 1950

The names under the photograph:
Gil Winters, Jack Bell, and "Red"—
is he the one in the tweed cap
who climbs, his dip net ready,
over the rocks above the river,
rocks like the prow of a boat?

I could make up stories about these men
or ask who they really were.
If the answer is my grandfather's
fishing friends, would I know anything?

Who can I ask? Everyone
in Shelburne County?
But would those on the other end
of the phone know the weather
that spring day at Jordan River
and how the wind sometimes
swooped low like a scavenging crow?

Who was the guide? Old photos
are hurricane lamps that cloud over
or stones blackened by the open fire.
Does Jordan River have any answers?

If Red scaled those rocks,
he stood there above the others
as if he had measured and tamed the wilderness.
Could be that all his life he never travelled
further south than Cape Sable,
never saw the city.

Maybe his father taught him
to cup his hands around his mouth,
shimmy his wrist—the resulting
sound a duck calling
        food's here, food
        is good.

Who is the guide?
White water swirls, steams
forward around the bend in the river.
It's a wing,
white feathers.

They caught eleven trout,
laid them out, jewels on the grass
with rod and woven creel.

I'm going to ask
no one, let the stories fly.

HALO

I

In the photograph they're awash
in butterscotch: mother and child,
the cabin in the café au lait
trees. They're sun-touched,
bronzed by balmy August.

It bathes the child, the dazzling
child perched on the verandah railing
in bloomers and sun bonnet,
her mother beside her
with an arm out—
to steady her,
to touch.

The child's aglow, relishing
her new height, almost grazing
the rafters, the broad *V*
of their open arms. They point to her,
catch a blazing sunburst—
this is her halo, my aunt
at five.

II

Five years later
the house lights go down,
a theatre darkens, and she,

among so many others, gazes up
at the newsreel, 1945—
                                        her falling
                                    to where
no one can catch her.

The pictures swallowing
words and light.

III

She dons the dark habit—

hush,
        float and whisper
of its folds—

enters the convent:
                            refuge.

AUNT DI BEFORE HER VOWS

She plants a birch log
in the fire: flames catch
scarred white bark and soar
before they wrap themselves
around wood grain.

A week at the cabin to answer
her last questions about giving
herself to God. She lifts

a trunk's heavy lid—under old blankets
a book opens, almost
by itself: the words
of the grandmother she never knew—

"to walk out into the water
and disappear."

The white pages that follow
so cleanly,
so pale, so much like the deer
on the Cape—

albino: shimmer, white smoke,
framed by dark trees—

who held her gaze
before the white flame,
before it quietly
turned its back.

TO NAME A BROOK

Naming a brook takes more
than sixty years, more than wintering
with Bigelows who timbered the mountain
where the brook flowed

for Glooscap's animal friends
who drank from the waters
parallel to the Borden brook
that runs behind the cabin
my father came to as a child.

Every summer and fall he returned
for work and the green world.

Naming takes knowing
its dedicated path, the woods
at the Cookhouse Turn
where he sawed logs for Jim and Bill
and fields where he hefted
fifty-pound potato bags with wind
coming in off the Basin.

The wind never named the brook
that he returned to later with his bride,
then built a cabin under the mountain;
blink of an old eye.

To name a brook takes several generations,
trees felled and pulled down the mountain
by horse. My father knows the history of these trees

and the family who has all
but disappeared
from the woods
where the Bigelow brook flows,
all seasons.

BRIDE

He brought his bride
to Blomidon, summer of '55
when the road was unpaved
and that last hill had you

—stomach riding
to the clouds—holding
on as you went steep
down, fender of the '52 Chevy
pointed at the Cape's full,
inscrutable face.

What did she make
of the camp's dark kitchen?
Did she expect to churn for water,
pump the rusty long elbow near the sink
and cook under the mantel's dusty cherub?

Verandah: in a black and white photo
she reclines on sun chair: lemon,
lime, and orange juice stripes
and she with no worries,
sunbathing, a woman on holiday.

Responsibility is a stick lying on the beach.
It drifted in; she tosses it away.

My mother before we are born.
A year later it drifts in again.
This time she grabs it, is ready.

HIS WORDS ABOUT THE BROOK

My father on an autumn day:

"I went back to the brook on the Cape where we watered the horses, and in winter, the cattle. The brook that Hun and Skip dammed to spray the Ben Davis and Ribston orchard during the war years.

Now I'll go back a hundred years or more to lands east of Scot's Bay, the Look Off—when Borden's Supply Company, 1899 cut fifteen million board feet: lumber sluiced down the mountain, down the brook half a mile to the landing. The *Millie K*, a tug, skippered by Bert Connors, Noble Blenkhorn, towed the boom to Kingsport. Clinton Bigelow cut the logs, rolled them over the fifty foot bank into the Minas Basin.

Old photos show these operations, and a thriving community, circa 1900. At the end of the first war, Borden sold land to Clinton, owner of Blomidon's first car, who milled at Ells Brook, on the Aberdeen Brook, the landing, back to Ells Brook in '27."

But old photos don't show the lean years,
the move to the quiet farm years,
and the quieter years of the park.
There's no photo of my father that autumn day
walking back to the brook, remembering—
or the following spring, his last,
when he wrote about the brook.

BEDTIME STORIES

Father reads us the story
of Chebec, the boy who worried tomorrow.

Can you hear tomorrow brewing
his spruce tea, slow boil and simmer,
see him stretching his legs?

The tea hasn't steeped twenty-four hours
when Chebec falls in love.
The girl's father says
    Sit, listen for the storm
    at the door of the high cliff
    where lives the giant Chenoo.
    He steals our brides, keeps
    his soul in a secret place.

Tomorrow with time to eavesdrop
throws his worry beads in the bay.
"Come up to the highest place,
son-in-law": Chebec is wed

as if time runs rabbit-fast
when we're not in Blomidon,
time, a white animal in winter,
is lost or caught in a trap.

Wind rush and wreck: the giant bellows,
snatches the bride as if he were squirrel
and she seed.

Chebec will rescue her now, worry tomorrow.

Three times he saves the animals
he meets: fish in a tangle of twigs,
caribou with antlers entwined in hawthorn,
and hawk in a rabbit snare.

Three times they say of their gifts:
fish scale, tuft of hair, feather—
"warm it with your hands
and we'll come."

Chebec fights conspiring wind and rain.

Then swish, rustle of great wings,
the largest goose settles beside him,
Glooscap to tell him *Stop*
and *Think* are animals as skilled as those
who answer—yes, Chebec considers—
soft pitapat, hill
over valley of his hands:

as the fish finds the key
in the box at the bottom
of the sea, as caribou's antlers
open it, as hawk flies to that far
mountaintop where a second box
holds the giant's soul, the pine cone

that Chebec squeezes—the giant
shrinks and runs far away.

THE SOUL OF THIS PLACE

The soul has shape, size, and colour
to the Wabanaki "who live where day breaks."
So what would they say of this place?

I'll venture it's larger than the long curve
and sweep, wanderlust of the Cape
that, winter-long, calls
when we're elsewhere.

Stretches its long arms
to us when we finally drive her way.
So large she can't help but peek
over restless hills.

I'll say it's shaped like words
in the log: Mom "puttering," loose
and as long as her hair
which she'll braid. Oh, the thick strands
and the hour's generosity.

It's in drawings: Dad "splitting wood"—
                she may have meant snoring,
                balmy snooze after lunch—
but her sketch of a round mountain
—shape and size repeating—
implying heft, the axe.

It's in that plummet, charged
and smithied slice, grey steel blade,
slim triangle—

thwack
on stump: wood, halved
and quartered, holds your soul.

Or part of it.
It's shaped and ripens
like apples, red cabbage that blooms,
sprawls across the field, multi-leaved
and layered, icy plum-
and grackle-fringed.

RESCUE BEFORE THE CABIN'S TORCHED

The summer visitors have gone
and the cabin's windows
have cataracts, the grey boards
like bones, arthritic,
about to break.

Arley, neighbour, takes a last look.
The delphinium always makes her think
of infinity or the oracle—
if those blue petals
could talk, they would moan
about a fate worse than winter:

matches,
                asphalt.

Maybe plants feel the future
like a mending bone can sense rain.

And inside—no fire, no furniture;
they've taken it all away
except for—

she spies a painting
above the generous stones
of the fireplace. Floral envelope
of white roses, sweet william,
wisteria, everlasting,
doctor foxglove, and chamomile—
they are more than perennial.
In her hands now
they will not burn.

BEFORE THE CABIN'S TORCHED

A chainsaw buzz and drone
with the scent of pine, work clothes,
the determined tree standing tall,
then that fulsome crack
before he hears it coming
straight toward him—

like the fluid roar a boy hears
in the Niagara River, then the silence,
the calm as he plunges over the falls.

Skip saying the cabin's goodbye,
thinking he might hear echoes
of the old folks, Gerald and Marjorie
in his parents' time.

He says, "She's a fish in Fundy,
time is and no one can catch her."
The men outside with matches, gasoline.

Then he hears it, that sound
as he turns, surrounded: flames
like alders growing tall around him,
thicket. The cabin so parched.

The sound that fire makes when it stands
like a bear on its hind legs
and roars. Before it rushes.
Before he finds the door.

THE VERANDAH STEPS

Is it important
that they're on the right
in '47, delphinium brimming
beside them, but by '58
have moved to the west side

as if they followed the sun
or the dog that quietly saunters
away, an actor disappearing offstage.

Is there any chronology or logic?
The meandering steps
like cows in a large pasture
or the tide undecided about where
it will turn. But it will.

Tell me where the steps were in '63
when my father, alone, wrote in the log,
"Apple blossoms are beautiful"

and in '66 when we arrived,
4:30 on July 15,
where were they then?
I don't remember
where my hand touched wood.

HAND-DRAWN MAPS

They are the lines of loyalty,
of my father's young life and the free
long afternoons he'd be fishing,
finding new trails, marking them
in his mind until he drew the trees
and fields, the path that, in autumn,
was leaf-strewn, a silent channel
through the silver-grey woods.

He knew how to stay downwind
of deer and step so that
twigs and leaves breathed
under the arch of his boot.

The maps are intimate affairs, affirmation
that hunting has no prize
but the quiet,
acute envelopment.

When he came out of the woods
he was reluctant to speak.

The blackened billy can:
testament to tea stewed so strong
it straightened turns in the road—
Netty's,
the reservoir, Sheep Pen,
and Cookhouse.

July ’67, the boys and Dad camped
on the Laid-Out Road: he’s drawn
three green clouds for alders, blue ripple
for the Borden Brook, sunburst
for fire. Deer trails are ripe arrows
fanning out beyond the Hardwood Forest
north of Roger’s Clear.

It’s time they quenched their thirst
at Ells Brook. He’s drawn
the pole and sinker hook
that will catch ten trout.

The maps are “we were here,”
teaching and holding
down the names and strange acres
like tent pegs—
tap them once with a rock,
and once more again.

HISTORY IN THOSE FIELDS

For years they had no names,
those who lived on the Cape.
History played hide-n-seek at twilight
and ran like a white-tailed deer.

It's true; we may not have cared
for her or she for us.

But fifty years on, I find
a notebook, her name—
top of the page as if she roams
those turn-of-the-century fields
in her long dress: rustle
and swish of black taffeta
past the pewter stones of their cellars:

Newton who begat Ames
and Henderson who begat Frank Porter.
Josh or Jim was blacksmith, Ames farmed
200 sheep and Nettie—sister?—
had a log house halfway up
at the hairpin turn
named for her.

Why did she live there? Dark wood
evening, morning's scramble to wash
in the falls. To whom or what
was she married? History's
her twin and they were shy girls.

And Rufus Jess—"chin wiskers"
says my father's note—
for five years he carried mail, trudged
from Canning to Blomidon, over
the bone-jarring, laid-out
log-rumbling road to Scot's Bay.

When wheels got stuck and he was thirsty
did he—could he—read the letters?
When he got home how soon
did he shave and wash off
the pitch and dust and tumult?

IN THE TURNING

A photograph: a year of the mountain;
someone drinking from a barrel,
mountain water soft, cold, an ancient taste.

Another photograph: a rusted field,
barrels full of earth and potatoes.
Next year the crops rotate.

In a turn on the mountain road,
the old potato barrel
hides itself behind the years:

where the Laid-Out Road
turns north to Scot's Bay
the mailman took his horse and buggy
across the mountain,
ten miles in the morning fog.

Where Netty had her house
close to the falls, now only the foundation
stone, a piece of pottery, her name.

And still the mountain water
hides in the turning.

SHE SPEAKS TO HER DROWNED MOTHER

Was the tide really going out?
Did you go to the beach to paint

or did the waters call?
Was it sudden

or did you linger in the camp
all those sad days?

Did it rain too much?
What other things fell away?

Did you think of calling
from the Bigelows at the bottom
of the field? Mary might have cooked for you.

Or were you in one of those moods
when your own voice

is shallow, like digging in the sand
for something you can't find

or wasn't there at all?
Did you make a fire at night?

Last night the plaster cherub
on the mantel puffed its round cheeks—

cloud of God—did, for a minute,
the fire burn more bright?

Did you eat the night before?
When you painted Milford:
the silver and greens of lakes—
did the canoe slip away
early morning from the dock?

When did you last go
onto that waterway and reel in trout?

There's a photograph Gerald took:
rocks and creel—you could have painted it.

Is it true that the talented suffer
like those fish?

Is the artist more prone?
Or is it our sex?

We go off to the drawing room
and the men to their cigars
and port. Politics is too cruel
for us but where can we speak our mind?

Do the ghosts of the drowned—
do they float? In your palette what colour
is melancholy? Could you not
paint it away?

P.S. The daughter I bore
after you walked out that morning
is sleeping well. I so would have liked
for you to see her.

A SACRED PLACE

She is a noble home—the Cape:
theatre of cliff,
sandstone throne:
Glooscap came in his stone canoe
to this, his chosen place.

She is a calendar of crops, milk
with more than a hint of pasture,
the first apple—superlatives
are her allies.

She's a topography
of winter and spring waiting
and that first drive, too many
restless stops before Canning,
Pereau with its deltas and mudflats,
Delhaven with the fields:
rolling temples, portals.

When we swim, Fundy is our watery altar.
When we camp, wood spirits guide us.
Nancy's pet raccoon in another life
had a Wabanaki name
and washed the Great Chief's food.

Tractors and plows are part
of the portrait,
the wharf rocks like totems
and there's truth in the land.

Where we play hide-and-go-seek,
we find more
than farmers' sons hiding in the woodpile,
behind the bunkhouse or barn.

When we toss hay bales, transcendental
farmland, we are at energy's crossroad:
sweep of wind to the cliff and beach—

After Sunday school, my sister
says, "We are lucky;
we have God and Glooscap"

though we are heathens
at Halloween under the grand elms.

Does everyone have their Glooscap's Lodge?
If they don't, how do they live?

BLOMIDON BEACH

Someday we'll walk around to Amethyst Cove,
find rocks that break smoothly
in our hands to reveal
darkness in rich amethyst.

Someday we'll walk around the Cape,
keep the tide back with wishing.

We'll go out at dusk to shallow water,
fill our pockets with dulse,
spread it out on the lawn next morning
and with starfish we'll make constellations.

We'll make beaches everywhere we go.

DELIBERATIONS, AT A CRAFT MARKET

For many years I fixed her on the beach:
leaning against bleached driftwood
with her oils and sketchbook,
her canvas: the terracotta vista,
approaching tide.

She's immersed
in the painterly, absorbing
preoccupation of colour and brush,
getting wet, inch
by oblivious inch.

But Di says no, wrapping
a carved heron in white paper.
Even wooden birds migrate.

December, taking stock of the years,
of her grandmother.
                                        One summer
Di found her journal.

December, the birds have flown,
these the months
of the missing.

She never saw those pages again—
they too drifted
deliberately—

so the extended family
of leavings, endings,
the lies of etiquette
and propriety's white gloves:

"heart attack . . . while bathing"
says the yellowed clipping,
Kentville, 1935.

"There will be no inquest."

NOTES

GLOOSCAP'S FIRE (PAGE 110)
Italicized phrases come from Kay Hill's *More Glooscap Stories: Legends of the Wabanaki Indians* (McClelland and Stewart, 1970).

TO NAME A BROOK (PAGES 127–28)
Italicized passages come from a proposal by David Dwyer to name a brook in Blomidon Provincial Park, a proposal to Kings County Council and the Province of Nova Scotia, November 2003.

BEDTIME STORIES (PAGES 131–32)
This poem is based on Kay Hill's story, "The Boy Who Worried Tomorrow," in *Glooscap and His Magic* (McClelland & Stewart, 1963).

ACKNOWLEDGEMENTS

I would like to thank the editors of the following magazines and anthologies that have published earlier versions of some of the poems from this collection:

Amethyst Review, *The Antigonish Review*, *CV2*, *The Dalhousie Review*, *Dandelion*, *Freefall*, *Germination*, *Grain*, *Landmarks: An Anthology of New Atlantic Canadian Poetry of the Land*, *The Malahat Review*, *Vallum*, and *Zygote*.

I would also like to thank the Halifax Poetry Group (Brian, Gen, Jill, John, Margo, Tonja, and especially Sue MacLeod) for their warm camaraderie, feedback, support, and visits. Much appreciation, friendship, and love goes to the folks of Lower Blomidon who welcomed us into their community. I would also like to thank the authors of the following books: Kay Hill for *Glooscap and His Magic* (Toronto: McClelland & Stewart, 1963) and *More Glooscap Stories: Legends of the Wabanaki Indians* (Toronto: McClelland & Stewart, 1970), and Esther Clark Wright for *Blomidon Rose* (Toronto: Ryerson Press, 1957). To Michael and all the crew at ECW for their generous help, and Emily, a big thank you for your kind attention to detail. To Laura MacDonald of Deep Hollow Print, a deep appreciation and gratitude for your artwork for the cover image.

Published by ECW Press
665 Gerrard Street East
Toronto, Ontario, Canada, M4M 1Y2
416-694-3348 / info@ecwpress.com

MISFIT

Editor for the press:
Michael Holmes/a misFit book
Cover design: Rachel Ironstone
Cover illustration: © Deep Hollow Print

Permissions: page i map of Blomidon scanned from a fragment pasted into one of the logbooks and believed to have been cut from a map issued by Natural Resources Canada; page ii–iii is from the Map of the Eastern Portion of British North America, by Henry F. Perley, circa 1853, now in the public domain

LIBRARY AND ARCHIVES CANADA
CATALOGUING IN PUBLICATION

Dwyer, Deirdre, author
The Blomidon logs / Deirdre Dwyer.

Poems.
Issued in print and electronic formats.
ISBN 978-1-77041-345-0 (paperback)
ALSO ISSUED AS: 978-1-77090-945-8 (PDF)
978-1-77090-944-1 (ePUB)

I. Title.

PS8557.W93B56 2016 C811'.54 C2016-902382-6
C2016-902383-4

The publication of *The Blomidon Logs* has been generously supported by the Canada Council for the Arts, which last year invested $153 million to bring the arts to Canadians throughout the country, and by the Government of Canada through the Canada Book Fund. *Nous remercions le Conseil des arts du Canada de son soutien. L'an dernier, le Conseil a investi 153 millions de dollars pour mettre de l'art dans la vie des Canadiennes et des Canadiens de tout le pays. Ce livre est financé en partie par le gouvernement du Canada.* We also acknowledge the support of the Ontario Arts Council (OAC), an agency of the Government of Ontario, which last year funded 1,737 individual artists and 1,095 organizations in 223 communities across Ontario for a total of $52.1 million, and the contribution of the Government of Ontario through the Ontario Book Publishing Tax Credit and the Ontario Media Development Corporation.

Ontario
Ontario Media Development Corporation

ONTARIO ARTS COUNCIL
CONSEIL DES ARTS DE L'ONTARIO
an Ontario government agency
un organisme du gouvernement de l'Ontario

Canada Council for the Arts
Conseil des Arts du Canada
Canada

PRINTED AND BOUND IN CANADA

PRINTING: COACH HOUSE 5 4 3 2 1